A small book of

JEWISH COMEDIANS

A small book of

JEWISH COMEDIANS

Introduction by Bobby Slayton
Edited by Tony Nourmand

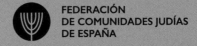

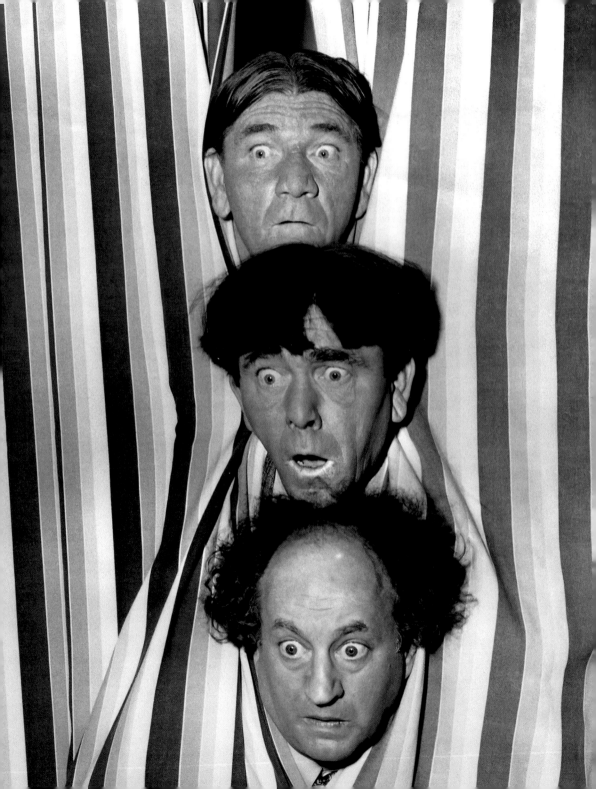

ABOUT THIS BOOK

This book is published in conjunction with the exhibition of Jewish Comedians at La Térmica Cultural Centre in Málaga, Spain, in November 2021. It is the first in a series of exhibitions and books celebrating Jewish culture in the arts.

The series is the brainchild of Salomon Castiel, head of La Térmica, and with the collaboration of La Federación de Comunidades Judías de España [The Federation of Jewish Communities of Spain]. The series is produced and curated in collaboration with Reel Art Press, London.

All photographs and accompanying quotes in this book are the editorial choices of Reel Art Press alone.

"IS BOBBY SLAYTON YOUR REAL NAME?"

"IS BOBBY SLAYTON YOUR REAL NAME?" I get that a lot, usually when I'm performing in Manhattan or South Florida where, coincidentally, there happens to be quite a large concentration of my people. And yes, it is my real name. Technically, of course, it's *Robert Slayton*, but for a future life in the comedy business, I thought Bobby just sounded better, although it seemed to work out fine for Robert Klein (who is also Jewish by the way). It's a question I am asked often, as so many performers altered their names when they ventured into the world of showbiz (and *not* just Jews, but let's keep with the theme of the book). Yacov Moshe Maza is a perfectly acceptable name if you're an Israeli Mossad agent but *not* for a comic. So Yacov changed his name to Jackie Mason. And, of course, many others Anglicized their names when they arrived in America. The only place I ever emigrated to was from New York to California. My father is a different story. While he had no aspirations for a career in Hollywood and was quite content (I think) supporting his family as a carpet salesman living in the Bronx, my mother told me she refused to marry him until he changed his name from Seymour Slutzkin. And no, I'm not making that up. My dad also told me he thought of taking my mother's maiden name—Klein—but then I would have been Robert Klein and would have had

to eventually change my name as well. So Slutzkin became Slayton. Whew ... close call.

Growing up in the suburbs of New York City in the '60s, my introduction and initiation to the world of stand-up comedy was probably from watching *The Ed Sullivan Show* on Sunday nights. While all the comics weren't Jewish, it certainly seemed that they dominated the field. I remember seeing so many of them—Alan King (Irwin Kniberg), Joan Rivers (Joan Molinsky), Woody Allen (Allen Stewart Konigsberg) and dozens more. Even as a small child, three of my favorite kiddie shows in New York were hosted by Paul Winchell (Paul Wilchinsky), Shari Lewis (Phyllis Naomi Hurwitz) and the legendary Soupy Sales (Milton Supman).

Every day after school, if my mother wasn't yelling at me to shut off "the idiot box" and go outside to play, I'd be watching *The Three Stooges* (all Jews coincidentally ...). A few years later when I was old enough to stay up later on weekends, there were reruns of *The Colgate Comedy Hour* with Jerry Lewis (Joseph Levitch), *Your Show of Shows* with Sid Caesar (Isaac Sidney Caesar) and, my favorite, *You Bet Your Life* with Groucho Marx (Julius Henry Marx). Surprise! All Jewish!

This book is a photo celebration of so many of the great Jewish humorists that have spent their lives making people laugh. There are plenty of other books and information on the web about the history of comedy that fully cover vaudeville, Las Vegas, the early days of film and television, and, of course, the Borscht Belt, often referred to as the *Jewish Alps* (that would be New York's Catskill Mountains for those of you who are not Jews or have never met one). This was all mostly before my time.

In 1977 when I started performing, the Catskills were pretty much over, and my act was a bit too *blue* and not nearly developed enough to open up for major headliners on the Vegas strip like many of my peers. But I relished hearing stories about the colorful mob-drenched days of Vegas from my friends David Brenner and Sammy Shore (more Jews!). Sammy was not only the founder of the world famous Comedy Store on the Sunset Strip but also took on the challenging and difficult task opening shows for Elvis Presley in Vegas. For some reason The King must have liked the traditional Borscht Belt style of stand-up because his other opening act, who traveled with him the last five years of his life, was Jackie Kahane, my first manager when I arrived in Los Angeles. Jackie was also responsible for landing me my national television debut on *Norm Crosby's Comedy Shop*. Norm and Jackie were both sweethearts, real old school comedians and, believe it or not, both Jewish!

After a few years working hard figuring out the stand-up racket, I was capable enough (and fast enough!) to open shows for many of the rock bands traveling through San Francisco. Plus the fact that most of the other comics who were working in the Bay Area were not in any hurry to take on this sometimes unenviable task. It was *kill or be killed* up on that stage. I always expected the worst. If I made it through my allotted time up there, didn't get booed off stage, had most of the crowd's attention and got a few laughs, I considered it a success. Kind of like riding the mechanical bull in a cowboy bar. Just stay on long enough to make your fifty bucks and get off. It's part of the reason I got the nickname *Yid Vicious*.

The first few times I got on a stage to try to make people laugh was at a very small club in San Francisco called the Holy City Zoo. I was 21 years old and also working part-time as a doorman at the Boarding House, an acclaimed music and comedy venue where both Steve Martin and Robin Williams worked regularly and *The King of One-Liners*, Henny Youngman, spent a whole week performing his Borscht Belt era nightclub act for a new generation of comedy fans. I was one of them. I had seen Henny on television growing up, but never in person doing a full hour in front of a live audience. A few months later I was at a party repeating his jokes to a small captive living room full of people when someone suggested I sign up for the open mic night at the Holy City Zoo. When I finally got the nerve to put together some material of my own and do it, I knew this was what I wanted to do with the rest of my life. And as much as I loved repeating his material, Henny's rapid one-liner delivery was certainly not the particular style of stand-up that I wanted to pursue. I wonder if I ever would have even attempted it had I not rattled off a couple of Youngman's jokes at that party and got a few laughs.

There were a bunch of other comics, many of them in this book, that also helped mold, develop, and influence my act. I'm sure watching David Brenner in the '70s and his ubiquitous declarations that often started with *You ever notice …?"* subconsciously paved the way for many of my own—and many young comics—observations. There was Milton Berle (Mendel Berlinger) busting my balls at a Friars Club roast for talking too fast, and lunches with Jan Murray (Murray Janovsky) at the Hillcrest Country Club suggesting I also slow down and maybe clean up my act a little. When I presented one of my biggest comedy heroes, Don Rickles, with a Lifetime Achievement Award at the Montreal Comedy Festival in 2014, he could not have been a nicer, funnier, classier human being, but also told me to please keep it clean when I introduced him.

I respected all of their opinions and critiques since these guys were such successful groundbreaking classic comedy warhorses who I admired tremendously and grew up watching, but when I repeated their comments to Buddy Hackett (Leonard Hacker) over bagels and lox at Nate'n Al's delicatessen in Beverly Hills, he said, *"Fuck them. Just do what you do and do it well."*

I loved them all and cherished the time I got to hang with them, but for what it's worth, Buddy is the one I really listened to.

I had heard of the venerable Lenny Bruce (Leonard Alfred Schneider) but didn't really know much about him until a few of the regular, more seasoned comics watching me flailing around on stage let me know that I should drop a few jokes from my act because Lenny Bruce had already done similar ones. After being told that, I became fascinated by Lenny and bought all of his records and books about his life and career. I didn't really see much of a similarity between our acts, especially since I'd only been dabbling in the comedy world a couple of months and Lenny had been an established brilliant performer fighting the good fight over the First Amendment and doing his damndest at the same time juggling social commentary while trying to make audiences laugh. I was just a young idiot trying to figure out *funny*. Of course, I dropped the bits attributed to Lenny, but at least felt a touch more secure that I was possibly headed in the right direction. I wound up dropping *another* joke a few months later when I saw Joey Bishop (Joseph Abraham Gottlieb) do the exact same one on television. Twenty years later HBO cast me to play Joey in the film *The Rat Pack*, where I wound up doing his material again anyway!

Enjoy the book and thanks for listening. And hopefully laughing a little bit.

BOBBY SLAYTON *(Robert Michael Slayton, b.1955)*

JEWISH COMEDIANS

A short summary of every Jewish holiday:
"They tried to kill us; we won; let's eat!"

—

Marriage is nature's way of keeping us
from fighting with strangers.

—

You do live longer with bran, but you spend
the last fifteen years on the toilet.

—

Why spoil a good meal with a big tip?

ALAN KING *(Irwin Alan Kniberg, 1927-2004)*

Had an unexplained burst of happiness today.
Doctor said not to worry, it will go away.

—

I'd still like to see "Survivor" minus the planned
show-biz parts. That would be the purest form of show
business. I want to see someone so hungry that
they eat somebody else's foot.

—

Being a screenwriter in Hollywood is like being
a eunuch at an orgy. Worse, actually ... at least
the eunuch is allowed to watch.

—

Excited about Black Friday.
Also excited about Jew Tuesday.

ALBERT BROOKS *(Albert Lawrence Einstein, b.1947)*

Success is like winning the sweepstakes
or getting killed in an automobile crash ...
it always happens to somebody else.

—

Grandma cheated whenever she could.
She cheated because it was a much more scientific
and surer way of winning than trusting to luck.

—

You want to fall in love with a shoe, go ahead.
A shoe can't love you back, but, on the other hand,
a shoe can't hurt you too deeply either.
And there are so many nice-looking shoes.

—

Adultery—which is the only grounds for divorce
in New York—is not grounds for divorce in California.
As a matter of fact, adultery in Southern California
is grounds for marriage.

ALLAN SHERMAN *(Allan Copelon, 1924-1973)*

*My mother sent me to psychiatrists since
the age of four because she didn't think little boys
should be sad. When my brother was born, I stared out
the window for days. Can you imagine that?*

—

*It's not that I was crazy. It's just that I was sad at times
because the world was sad at times. When I would
perform, it wasn't sad anymore.*

—

*The more they hate you,
the better you're doing.*

—

I never told a joke in my life.

ANDY KAUFMAN *(Andrew Geoffrey Kaufman, 1949-1984)*

*I married a German. Every night I dress up
as Poland and he invades me.*

—

*When it's three o'clock in New York,
it's still 1938 in London.*

—

*I have my standards. They're low,
but I have them.*

—

*I've always said we got married
because there was nothing on TV.*

BETTE MIDLER *(Bette Davis Midler, b.1945)*

I was raised half-Jewish and half-Catholic. When I'd go to confession, I'd say, "Bless me, Father, for I have sinned … and you know my attorney, Mr. Cohen.

—

The thing I don't understand about homosexuals is, how do they decide which one is the one who's supposed to pretend they don't want it?

—

You know … there is a name for people who are always wrong about everything all the time … husband!

—

All across the Middle East in the streets, people are demanding democracy. It's amazing. The only way in America you get people to get worked up like that is to threaten to give them health care.

BILL MAHER *(William Maher, b.1956)*

Women need a reason to have sex.
Men just need a place.

—

At 60, I could do the same things I could do at 30,
if I could only remember what those things are.

—

From the first time I saw Sid Caesar be funny
I knew that's what I had to do.

—

(My family are) the kind of people who spoke mostly
Yiddish, which is a combination of German and
phlegm. This is a language of coughing and spitting;
until I was eleven, I wore a raincoat.

BILLY CRYSTAL *(William Edward Crystal, b.1948)*

I would probably be a teacher
if I weren't a comedian. Humor is healing.

—

It's all I have left in my life, caffeine and a poodle.

—

I think we love watching people
who are flawed because we are all flawed.

—

You have a bad day at the office,
four people know. You suck in a movie,
everyone knows.

BRAD GARRETT *(Bradley Henry Gerstenfeld, b.1960)*

I found out that if you made people laugh, they like you. Most people got to like me because I made them laugh. When they didn't, I hit them.

—

My wife said to me, "I want to be cremated." I said, "How about Tuesday?"

—

Golf is more fun than walking naked in a strange place but not much.

—

As a child my family's menu consisted of two choices: take it or leave it.

BUDDY HACKETT *(Leonard Hacker, 1924-2003)*

Every morning, I would actually look at the obituaries before I had breakfast. And as a joke I said if I was not in it, I would have the breakfast.

—

The absolute truth is the thing that makes people laugh.

—

A lot of people like snow. I find it to be an unnecessary freezing of water.

—

Comedians are really writers who don't have pens and pencils about them, but they riff.

CARL REINER *(Carl Reiner, 1922-2020)*

I wasn't born a fool.
It took work to get this way.

—

You bet I arrived overnight. Over a few hundred
nights in the Catskills, in vaudeville,
in clubs and on Broadway.

—

An unemployed jester is nobody's fool.

—

After all is said and done, it's usually the wife
who has said it and the husband who has done it.

DANNY KAYE *(David Daniel Kaminsky, 1911-1987)*

I was on a date with this really hot model. Well, it really wasn't a date. We just ate dinner and saw a movie. Then the plane landed.

—

Remember when you're young and you think your dad is Superman? Then you grow up and realize he's just a drunk who wears a cape.

—

*I gotta stop smoking, doctor's orders.
And the drinking, court orders.*

—

So, I travel a lot. I hate traveling, mostly because my dad used to beat me with a globe.

DAVE ATTELL *(David Attell, b.1965)*

I want my tombstone to read:
If this is a joke, I don't get it.

—

When I go to a bar, I don't go looking for
a girl who knows the capital of Maine.

—

I don't like watching golf on television
because I don't like people who whisper.

—

You know you're getting old when you
start to dress in more than six colors.

DAVID BRENNER *(David Norris Brenner, 1936-2014)*

The only reason I feel guilty about
masturbation is because I do it so badly.

—

My father never lived to see his dream
come true of an all-Yiddish-speaking Canada.

—

Silences are the most underrated part of comedy.

—

I used to have a theory, actually, that
if you've had a good childhood, a good marriage
and a little bit of money in the bank,
you're going to make a lousy comedian.

DAVID STEINBERG *(David Steinberg, b.1942)*

Don't call me "Sir"; "King Jew" will do fine.

—

I think if I took therapy, the doctor would quit.
He'd just pick up the couch and walk out of the room.

—

Italians are fantastic people, really;
they can work you over in an alley
while singing an opera.

—

I'm always afraid that somewhere out there,
there is one person in the audience
that I'm not going to offend!

DON RICKLES *(Donald Jay Rickles, 1926-2017)*

Is that your wife? ... Oh, well, keep your chin up.

—

If I were to insult people and mean it,
that wouldn't be funny.

—

Political correctness? In my humor,
I never talk about politics.
I was never much into all that.

—

No matter where you go in this world,
you will always find a Jew
sitting in the beach chair next to you.

DON RICKLES *(Donald Jay Rickles, 1926-2017)*

A comic says funny things.
A comedian says things funny.

—

A bachelor is a man who never
makes the same mistake once.

—

Every radish I pulled up seemed to
have a mortgage attached to it.

—

A comedian is not a man who opens a funny door.
He opens a door funny.

ED WYNN *(Isaiah Edwin Leopold, 1886-1966)*

When I see the Ten Most Wanted lists, I always
have this thought: If we'd made them feel wanted
earlier, they wouldn't be wanted now.

—

A wedding is a funeral where you
smell your own flowers.

—

Marriage is an attempt to solve problems
together which you didn't even have when
you were on your own.

—

He hasn't an enemy in the world—
but all his friends hate him.

EDDIE CANTOR *(Isidore Itzkowitz, 1892-1964)*

My ancestors wandered lost in the wilderness for 40 years because even in biblical times, men would not stop to ask for directions.

—

There's only one difference between Catholics and Jews; Jews are born with guilt, and Catholics have to go to school to learn it.

—

My brother is gay and my parents don't care, as long as he marries a doctor.

—

I know what men want; men want to be really, really close to someone who will leave them alone.

ELAYNE BOOSLER *(Elayne Boosler, b.1952)*

I'm a bad woman,
but I'm damn good company.

—

Love is like a card trick. After you
know how it works, it's no fun anymore.

—

I'm a bagel on a plate full of onion rolls.

—

For ten thousand dollars,
I'd endorse an opium pipe.

FANNY BRICE *(Fania Borach, 1891-1951)*

*Children are the most desirable opponents
at Scrabble as they are both easy to beat
and fun to cheat.*

—

*The opposite of talking isn't listening.
The opposite of talking is waiting.*

—

*To put it rather bluntly, I am not the type
who wants to go back to the land; I am the
type who wants to go back to the hotel.*

—

*Original thought is like original sin:
both happened before you were born
to people you could not have possibly met.*

FRAN LEBOWITZ *(Frances Ann Lebowitz, b.1950)*

The food in this restaurant is awful!
And such small portions!

—

An elderly couple goes on their honeymoon.
She went to bed first and yells downstairs to her new
husband, "Would you like to come upstairs and make
love?" He calls back, "I can't do both!"

—

Eleven years ago I became president for two
years [of the Friar's Club]. I'm like Fidel Castro.
I'm president for life.

—

Mike Tyson is an interesting story.
He's the only person in America who's driving
a $250,000 car who actually made
the license plates for that car.

FREDDIE ROMAN *(Fred Kirschenbaum, b.1937)*

My friends tell me I have an intimacy problem,
but they don't really know me.

—

I went to my doctor and told him,
"My penis is burning." He said,
"That means somebody is talking about it."

—

I told my girlfriend that unless she expressed her
feelings and told me what she liked I wouldn't be able
to please her, so she said, "Get off me."

—

I'm dating a homeless woman.
It was easier talking her into staying over.

GARRY SHANDLING *(Garry Emmanuel Shandling, 1849-2016)*

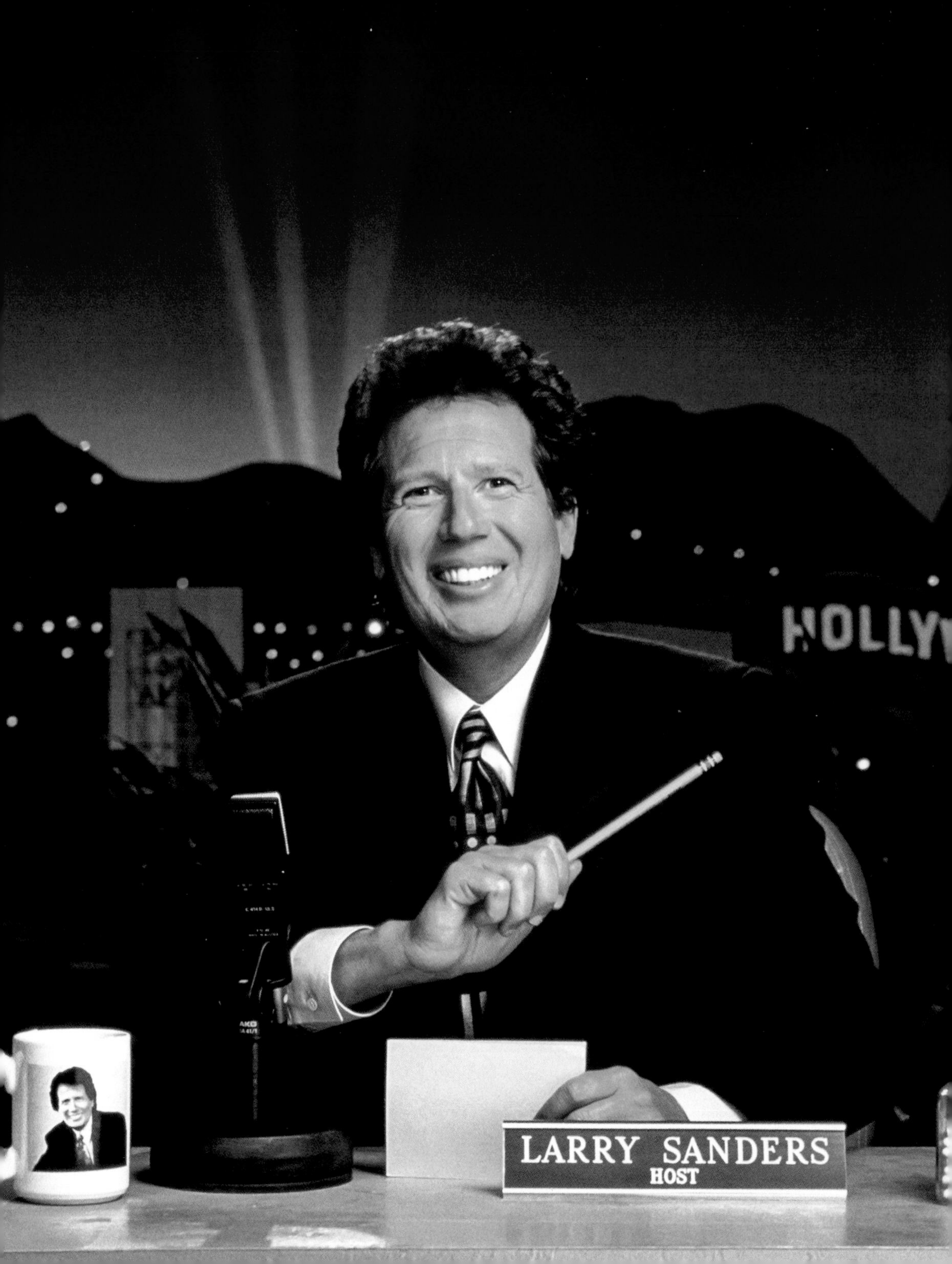
HOLLYW
LARRY SANDERS
HOST

After making love I said to my girl, "Was it good for you too?" And she said, "I don't think this was good for anybody."

—

I'm too shy to express my sexual needs except over the phone to people I don't know.

—

I once made love for an hour and fifteen minutes, but it was the night the clocks are set ahead.

—

I'm very loyal in relationships. Even when I go out with my mom, I don't look at other moms.

GARRY SHANDLING *(Garry Emmanuel Shandling, 1849-2016)*

Sex at 90 is like trying to shoot pool with a rope.

—

*Happiness is having a large, loving, caring,
close-knit family … in another city.*

—

When I was a boy, the Dead Sea was only sick.

—

*Do you know what it means to come home
at night to a woman who'll give you a little love,
a little affection, a little tenderness?
… It means you're in the wrong house,
that's what it means.*

GEORGE BURNS *(Nathan Birnbaum, 1896-1996)*

*Marriage is a mistake every
man should make.*

—

*If you don't strike oil in three
minutes, stop boring.*

—

*The human brain is a wonderful organ.
It starts to work as soon as you are born
and doesn't stop until you get up
to deliver a speech.*

—

*A toastmaster is a man who eats
a meal he doesn't want so he can get up
and tell a lot of stories he doesn't remember
to people who've already heard them.*

GEORGE JESSEL *(George Albert "Georgie" Jessel, 1898-1981)*

*I wanted to be a brain surgeon,
but I had a bad habit of dropping things.*

—

*I would show up at a party for Al Qaeda
if you said there's going to be a dinner.*

—

*If someone else is paying for it,
food just tastes a lot better.*

—

*I can't even find someone for a platonic
relationship, much less the kind where
someone wants to see me naked.*

GILBERT GOTTFRIED *(Gilbert Jeremy Gottfried, b.1955)*

*What's all this fuss I've been hearing about the presidential **erection**?*

—

*What's all this talk about the Supreme Court decision on a **deaf** penalty?*

—

*What's all this talk I've been hearing about **violins** on television?*

—

*What's all this talk I've been hearing about **busting** school children?*

GILDA RADNER *(Gilda Susan Radner, 1946-1989)*

All people are born alike—
except Republicans and Democrats.

—

I never forget a face, but in your case,
I'll be glad to make an exception.

—

Anyone who says he can see
through women is missing a lot.

—

I've had a perfectly wonderful evening.
But this wasn't it.

GROUCHO MARX *(Julius Henry Marx, 1890-1977)*

A hooker stopped me on the street and told me
"I'll do anything for $50." I said, "Paint my house."

—

A car hit a Jewish man. The paramedic says,
"Are you comfortable?" The man says,
"I make a good living."

—

A Polish terrorist was sent to blow up a car.
He burned his mouth on the exhaust pipe!

—

Why do Jewish men die before their wives?
They want to.

HENNY YOUNGMAN *(Henry Youngman 1906-1998)*

A man goes to a psychiatrist ... "Nobody listens to me!" The doctor says, "Next!"

—

I take my wife everywhere, but she keeps finding her way back.

—

A man goes to a psychiatrist. The doctor says "You're crazy." The man says, "I want a second opinion!" — "Okay, you're ugly too!"

—

My wife and I were happy for twenty years. Then we met.

HENNY YOUNGMAN *(Henry Youngman 1906-1998)*

Hors d'oeuvre: A ham sandwich
cut into forty pieces.

—

Age is strictly a case of mind over matter.
If you don't mind, it doesn't matter.

—

I went to a meeting for premature ejaculators.
I left early.

—

I practice three hours daily on my violin
so I won't get worse.

JACK BENNY *(Benjamin Kubelsky, 1894-1974)*

A guy complained to me his factory just burned down.
I asked him what he manufactured,
he said "good luck charms."

—

Never go to a high school reunion because
you will meet dead people that are still alive.

—

I'm starting to put rolls in my pocket after dinner.
Jews have a fear of dying of hunger in
the middle of the night.

—

"Why can't our sex life be like it was ten years ago?"
... "Because the maid quit, that's why."

JACK CARTER *(Jack Chakrin, 1922-2015)*

JACK E. LEONARD

*There's nothing wrong with you that
reincarnation won't cure.*

—

*My wife can answer all the questions on all the quiz
shows but can't remember what she did with
the money I gave her yesterday.*

—

*I figured out the other day how to lose 140 pounds.
I got rid of my mother-in-law.*

—

*Let's play horse—I'll be the front end,
and you just be yourself.*

JACK E. LEONARD *(Leonard Lebitsky, 1910-1973)*

*Eighty percent of married men cheat in America.
The rest cheat in Europe.*

—

*Did you know that the Jews invented sushi?
That's right—two Jews bought a restaurant
with no kitchen.*

—

*If an Englishman gets run down by a
truck he apologizes to the truck.*

—

*A Jew never laughs without looking at
his wife for approval.*

JACKIE MASON *(Yacov Moshe Maza, b.1931)*

Dieting: A system of starving yourself
to death so you can live a little longer.

—

Chubby Checker lost pounds by demonstrating
how to move as if you were drying
your back with a towel.

—

Sorry I'm late. That stupid wife of mine.
She didn't shovel the snow from the driveway this
morning. She also forgot to put on the snow tires.
And halfway to New York, I realized
she hadn't dressed me.

—

Until I was 80, I wasn't exhausted.
There's no medicine like being on
stage hearing people laugh.

JAN MURRAY *(Murray Janofsky, 1916-2006)*

I've had great success being a total idiot.
I get paid for what most kids get punished for.

—

You might as well like yourself; just think
about all the time you're gonna spend with you.

—

Comedy is a man in trouble. And without it,
there's no humor.

—

I'm taking Lasix, which makes me pee sometimes
seven, eight, eleven, twelve times.
I've decided to keep my fly open all day.

JERRY LEWIS *(Joseph Levitch, 1926-2017)*

If a book about failures doesn't sell,
is it a success?

—

Men want the same thing from their
underwear that they want from women:
a little bit of support, and a little bit of freedom.

—

Sometimes the road less traveled is
less traveled for a reason.

—

My parents didn't want to move to Florida,
but they turned sixty and that's the law.

JERRY SEINFELD *(Jerome Allen Seinfeld, b.1954)*

*Never go for the punchline. There might
be something funnier on the way.*

—

*Hollywood never knew there was a Vietnam War
until they made the movie.*

—

*My mother and father—I figured if I could make them
laugh, they'd stop fighting. I stole all their material.*

—

*I've got a prostate the size of a honeydew,
and a head full of bad memories.*

JERRY STILLER *(Gerald Isaac Stiller, 1927-2020)*

It was a Jewish porno film …
one minute of sex and nine minutes of guilt.

—

I don't exercise. If God had wanted me to bend over,
he would have put diamonds on the floor.

—

Half of all marriages end in divorce—
and then there are the really unhappy ones.

—

I wish I had a twin, so I could know what
I'd look like without plastic surgery.

JOAN RIVERS *(Joan Alexandra Molinsky, 1933-2014)*

I said to my husband, "My boobs have gone, my stomach's gone, say something nice about my legs". He said, "Blue goes with everything."

—

My mother could make anybody feel guilty— she used to get letters of apology from people she didn't even know.

—

My daughter and I are very close. We speak every single day and I call her every day and I say the same thing, "Pick up, I know you're there." And she says the same thing back, "How'd you get this new number?"

—

It's been so long since I made love I can't even remember who gets tied up.

JOAN RIVERS *(Joan Alexandra Molinsky, 1933-2014)*

Show me a friend in need,
and I'll show you a pest.

—

I drink to forget I drink.

—

You are only young once, and if you work
it right, once is enough.

—

I know a lot more old drunks
than old doctors.

JOE E. LEWIS *(Joseph Klewan, 1902-1971)*

You know how Van Nuys got its name? Well, one day my little old Jewish mother was visiting me, and I took her to the top of the Hollywood Hills and had her view the valley below just at sunset. "Well, mama, what would you call that?" And she said, "Ver nize."

—

I once called my mother during a hurricane. She got on the phone and said, "I can't talk to you, Joey, the lines are down."

—

Today you can go to a gas station and find the cash register open and the toilets locked. They must think toilet paper is worth more than money.

—

Last week I gave Dean Martin a cigarette lighter. He finished it in one gulp.

JOEY BISHOP *(Joseph Abraham Gottlieb, 1918-2007)*

I celebrated Thanksgiving in an old-fashioned way.
I invited everyone in my neighborhood to my house,
we had an enormous feast, and then
I killed them and took their land.

—

Yes, reason has been a part of organized religion,
ever since two nudists took dietary
advice from a talking snake.

—

You wonder sometimes how our government
puts on its pants in the morning.

—

No matter what your race, creed or sexual preference,
there is a word that people use to describe
you that is very nasty. It's what we all have
in common. That, and masturbation.

JON STEWART *(Jonathan Stuart Leibowitz, b.1962)*

Women love a self-confident bald man.

—

You know who wears sunglasses inside?
Blind people and assholes.

—

I had a wonderful childhood, which is tough because
it's hard to adjust to a miserable adulthood.

—

Switzerland is a place where they don't like to fight,
so they get people to do their fighting for them while
they ski and eat chocolate.

LARRY DAVID *(Lawrence Gene David, b.1947)*

*Never trust a preacher with
more than two suits.*

—

*The liberals can understand everything
but people who don't understand them.*

—

Life is a four-letter word.

—

*A lot of people say to me, "Why did you kill Christ?"
I dunno ... it was one of those parties
that got out of hand.*

LENNY BRUCE *(Leonard Alfred Schneider, 1925-1966)*

Republicans have nothing but bad ideas,
and Democrats have no ideas.

—

I like coffee because it gives me the illusion
that I might be awake.

—

Oh, sure I have regrets, but that's the nice
thing about age. Regrets fade, and eventually you die.

—

In New York, fuck isn't even a word.
It's a comma.

LEWIS BLACK *(Lewis Niles Black, b.1948)*

I'm not for everyone. I'm barely for me.

—

Buying my wife a gun is sort of like me saying,
"You know, I kinda want to kill myself,
but I want it to be a surprise."

—

It's easy to maintain your integrity when
no one is offering to buy it out.

—

For my next trick, I will make
everyone understand me.

MARC MARON *(Marc David Maron, b.1963)*

I've been accused of vulgarity.
I say that's bullshit.

—

Tragedy is when I cut my finger. Comedy is
when you fall into an open sewer and die.

—

If God wanted us to fly,
he would have given us tickets.

—

If presidents can't do it to their wives,
they do it to their country.

MEL BROOKS *(Melvin Kaminsky, b.1926)*

All my wife wanted for Valentine's Day
was a little card—American Express.

—

Anytime a person goes into a delicatessen
and orders a pastrami on white bread,
somewhere a Jew dies.

—

My wife calls our waterbed the Dead Sea.

—

Jews don't drink much because
it interferes with their suffering.

MILTON BERLE *(Mendel Berlinger, 1908-2002)*

*People who live in glass houses might as
well answer the door.*

—

*A cannibal is a person who walks into
a restaurant and orders a waiter.*

—

*According to statistics, a man eats a prune every
twenty seconds. I don't know who this man is,
but I know where to find him.*

—

*Our congress is the finest body
of men money can buy.*

MOREY AMSTERDAM *(Moritz Amsterdam, 1908-1996)*

Most people past college age are not atheists.
It's too hard to be in society, for one thing.
Because you don't get any days off. And if
you're an agnostic you don't know
whether you get them off or not.

—

Liberals feel unworthy of their possessions;
conservatives feel they deserve
everything they've stolen.

—

If you were the only person left on the planet,
I would have to attack you. That's my job.

—

There are Russian spies here now.
And if we're lucky, they'll steal some of our
secrets and they'll be two years behind.

MORT SAHL *(Morton Lyon Sahl, b.1927)*

Old is when people compliment your alligator shoes and you're not wearing any.

—

My school was so tough the school newspaper had an obituary section.

—

If your eyes hurt after you drink coffee, you have to take the spoon out of the cup.

—

When you go into court you are putting your fate into the hands of twelve people who weren't smart enough to get out of jury duty.

NORM CROSBY *(Norman Lawrence Crosby, 1927-2020)*

Be funny on a golf course?
Do I kid my best friend's mother
about her heart condition?

—

Vaudeville was an exhilarating, great new world
for me. It had its share of deadbeats and egocentric
maniacs and joke-snatchers. But we had warmth and
camaraderie and time for laughs.

—

Treat acting as a business and don't
let it go to your head. You don't want to
end up like my friends.

—

I only smile in public. When I'm alone, I just sort of
stare. People know we actors are frightened. And
when they read this, they'll know that I'm depressed.

PHIL SILVERS *(Philip Silver, 1911-1985)*

Ben Hur, who said to his sister Ben Him,
"We'd better swap names before
they start calling me Ben Gay!"
Never got a dinner!

—

Maid Marion, who said to Robin Hood,
"I will not live in a house with a Little John."
Never got a dinner!

—

Jack the Ripper's mother, who said to Jack,
"How come I never see you with the same girl twice?"
Never got a dinner!

—

Cain, whose wife divorced him
because he wasn't Able.
Never got a dinner!

RED BUTTONS *(Aaron Chwatt, 1919-2006)*

I tried phone sex and got an ear infection.

—

My grandmother was a Jewish juggler:
she used to worry about six things at once.

—

Most Texans think Hanukkah
is some sort of duck call.

—

I'm great in bed when I'm alone.

RICHARD LEWIS *(Richard Philip Lewis, b.1947)*

I love being married. It's so great
to find that one special person you
want to annoy for the rest of your life.

—

I read recipes the same way
I read science fiction. I get to the end and
say to myself, well that's not going to happen.

—

My grandmother was a very tough woman.
She buried three husbands and two
of them were just napping.

—

If your husband has trouble getting
to sleep, the words "We need to talk about
our relationship" might help.

RITA RUDNER *(Rita Rudner, b.1953)*

I was a class clown. My father was a class clown.
My son has been a class clown, and
it sort of ran in the family.

—

I'm not against profanity. It's an important part of the
language when used properly.

—

I was in the De Witt Clinton High School marching
band. One of the worst bands ever formed. When we
played the national anthem, people from every country
stood—except Americans.

—

In the fifties I had dreams about touching
a naked woman and she would turn to bronze,
or the dream about a hot dog chasing donuts
through the Lincoln Tunnel.

ROBERT KLEIN *(Robert Klein, b.1942)*

*When I was born I was so ugly the doctor
slapped my mother.*

—

*I bought a new Japanese car.
I turned on the radio …
I don't understand a word they're saying.*

—

*My cousin is gay; he went to London only
to find out that Big Ben was a clock.*

—

*I looked up my family tree and found
three dogs using it.*

RODNEY DANGERFIELD *(Jacob Rodney Cohen, 1921-2004)*

I'm taking Viagra and drinking prune juice—
I don't know if I'm coming or going.

—

I drink too much. The last time I gave a urine
sample it had an olive in it.

—

Terrible neighborhood. The first day I moved in, I
asked a cop, "How long a walk to the subway?"
He said, "I don't know, so far no one ever made it."

—

Went to a bar for a few drinks. The bartender
asked what I wanted. "Surprise me," I said. So he
showed me a naked picture of my wife.

RODNEY DANGERFIELD *(Jacob Rodney Cohen, 1921-2004)*

I'm not upset about my divorce;
I'm only upset I'm not a widow.

—

Women complain about premenstrual syndrome,
but I think of it as the only time of the month
that I can be myself.

—

People say to me, "You're not feminine."
Well, they can just suck my dick.

—

In Tulsa, restaurants have signs that say,
"Sorry, we're open."

ROSEANNE BARR *(Roseanne Cherrie Barr, b. 1952)*

I'm Jewish, but I'm totally not.

—

I don't care if you think I'm racist.
I just want you to think I'm thin.

—

People who call themselves divas …
you are not a diva. I'm pretty sure you're a cunt.

—

Once I was with two men in one night,
but I could never do it again—
I could hardly walk afterwards.
Two dinners. That's a lot of food.

SARAH SILVERMAN *(Sarah Kate Silverman, b.1970)*

Normally in dangerous situations
I have a getaway car.

—

Sex can lead to nasty things like herpes,
gonorrhea, and something called relationships.

—

Thank you to every American who has not
sued me so far.

—

Is it cos I is black?

SACHA BARON COHEN *(Sacha Noam Baron Cohen, b.1971)*

Frank Sinatra saved my life once. He said,
"Okay, boys. That's enough."

—

I lost $32,000 in the coffee shop waiting
for a bagel. I was playing Keno.

—

I have a daughter who goes to SMU.
She could've gone to UCLA here in California,
but it's one more letter she'd have to remember.

—

I had a silent partner to support.
I learned how to bet on the horses.

SHECKY GREENE *(Fred Sheldon Greenfield, b.1926)*

*A hotel is a place that keeps the manufacturers
of 25-watt bulbs in business.*

—

*I heard the other day of a man who paid
a psychologist $50 to cure him of an inferiority
complex—and was later fined $25 and costs
for talking back to a traffic cop.*

—

*Unquestionably, standup comedy
is and has always been an art form.*

—

*The old problems—love, money, security, health, etc.—
are still here to plague us or please us.*

SHELLEY BERMAN *(Sheldon Leonard Berman, 1925-2017)*

The guy who invented the first wheel was an idiot.
The guy who invented the other three,
he was a genius.

—

Comedy has to be based on truth.
You take the truth and you put a little
curlicue on the end.

—

The best thing about humor
is that it reminds people they are not alone.

—

If you can't stand yourself,
neither can anybody else.

SID CAESAR *(Isaac Sidney Caesar, 1922-2014)*

Hey, kids! I want you to tiptoe into your parents
bedrooms, look in their pockets for all the
green pieces of paper with the pictures of the
guys in beards, and send them to Soupy Sales
at Channel 5 in New York.

—

Be true to your teeth and they
won't be false to you.

—

If I had my life to live over,
I'd live it over a deli.

—

I took my wife to a baseball game.
I kissed her on the strikes, and
she kissed me on the balls.

SOUPY SALES *(Milton Supman, 1926-2009)*

Honesty is the best policy,
but insanity is a better defense.

—

I work a lot of colleges. And every college has a
football team. And there's always a guy named Moose.
You don't hear of a lot of dentists named Moose.

—

When I went back to visit my mother recently
I was really tired and she asked me if anything was
wrong. I said it could be anything—I'm Jewish.

—

There doesn't seem to be any
Jewish country singers.

STEVE LANDESBERG *(Stephen Landesberg, 1936-2010)*

*I've been on a diet for two weeks
and all I've lost is two weeks.*

—

*Happiness is getting a brown gravy
stain on a brown dress.*

—

*I've waited all my life to say this …
I weigh less than Elizabeth Taylor.*

—

*I exercise daily to keep my figure.
I keep patting my hand against
the bottom of my chin. It works too.
I have the thinnest fingers in town.*

TOTIE FIELDS (*Sophie Feldman, 1930-1978*)

51

I can levitate birds. No one cares.

—

*I failed to make the chess team
because of my height.*

—

*Life doesn't imitate art,
it imitates bad television.*

—

*There are worse things in life than death.
Have you ever spent an evening with
an insurance salesman?*

WOODY ALLEN *(Allan Stewart Konigsberg, b.1935)*

I wanted to say something about the universe.
There's God, angels, plants ... and horseshit.

—

The freedom of any society varies
proportionately with the volume of its laughter.

—

Romanian-Yiddish cooking has killed
more Jews than Hitler.

—

The heart is, truly, the source of love.
The proof is that if you remove it from someone,
they will almost certainly never love again.

ZERO MOSTEL *(Samuel Joel Mostel, 1915-1977)*

INDEX

ACKNOWLEDGEMENTS

Bobby Slayton would like to thank: my friend, and comedy historian, Jeff Abraham for all his suggestions. And John Kisch for his suggestions with my introduction.

Reel Art Press would like to thank: Salomon Castiel, Toni Garcia, Andy Howick at MPTV Images and Billie Woods Kisch. Special thanks to John Kisch for making *The Connection*.

PHOTO CREDITS

Introduction:	Bobby Slayton
Editor:	Tony Nourmand
Art Director:	Graham Marsh
Deputy Art Director:	Jack Cunningham
Managing Editor:	Alison Elangasinghe
Pre-Press:	HR Digital Solutions

First published 2021 by Reel Art Press, an imprint of Rare Art Press Ltd., London, UK

Published in conjunction with the exhibition of Jewish Comedians at La Térmica Cultural Centre in Málaga, Spain, in November 2021

reelartpress.com
latermicamalaga.com
fcje.org

First Edition 10 9 8 7 6 5 4 3 2 1

ISBN: 978-1-909526-83-9

Printed by Graphius, Gent